Notable Children's Books 82

A Duckling is Born

The photographs on pages 16 and 17 are by Claude Nardin/Jacana
Thanks are also due to Professor J. Schowing and his colleagues at
the Institut für Embryologie and Teratologie der Universität
Fribourg for their help with the photographs on pages 22–25.
First American edition 1981
Printed in the United States of America.
First impression.
Library of Congress Cataloging in Publication Data
Isenbart, Hans-Heinrich
A duckling is born.
Translation of: Ein Entchen kommt zur Welt.
Summary: Follows the development of a mallard
duckling from the mating of his parents to his first
swim, less than an hour after birth.
1. Mallard—Juvenile literature. 2. Embryology—Birds—Juvenile literature.
3. Animals, Infancy of—Juvenile literature. [1. Mallard. 2. Ducks.
3. Animals—Infancy] I. Baumli, Othmar II. Title.
QL696.A52I7313   5984′1   81–5205   AACR2
ISBN 0–399–20778–3

A Duckling is Born

by Hans-Heinrich Isenbart/photographs by Othmar Baumli

translation by Catherine Edwards Sadler

G. P. Putnam's Sons   New York

As winter approaches, male ducks like this familiar mallard grow their beautiful bright new feathers. Ducks are seen in the city, the country, on rivers and alongside lakes.

Among the many families of ducks are the teal, pintail, shoveler and mallard. In each family the male is called a drake, the female a duck.

This drake is showing off his shiny new feathers. He puffs up his chest proudly. He has his bright feathers for eight months of the year. During the summer his wing and tail feathers moult, or fall out, and he cannot fly. In the fall he moults a second time. Then his splendid full plumage grows in.

Now it is winter and the drake's colors are their most beautiful. He swims along looking for a mate. He makes a soft whistling sound—"yeeb, yeeb."

When he sees a young brown female nearby, he beats his wings to make her notice him. But another drake has seen the duck too.

Both drakes swim toward the duck and a fight breaks out. Finally one of the drakes is driven off.

Now, courtship begins, although the drake will have to fight off other drakes before he and the duck settle down to spend the winter together.

The plain brown feathers of the duck are not so colorful and bright as the drake's. But her plain colors are important. They blend into the background and hide her from enemies when she sits on her eggs in the nest.

Now the ducks spend all their time together. They look for food together, they swim together, and they groom themselves by rubbing oil from an oil gland at the back of their tails onto their feathers to make them waterproof. They look for food just below the surface of the water. They like to eat plants, tadpoles and small frogs that live there.

Sometimes they leave the water and fly high above the meadows and fields in search of food. But they always return to the water. The sound of their contented quacking can be heard just before they fall asleep.

When winter ends, it is time for the pair to mate. The drake holds the duck gently by the neck as he fertilizes the eggs growing inside her. Only when the eggs are fertilized by the drake will ducklings begin to grow inside the eggs.

Next the pair look for a good place to build their nest. The nest must be sheltered and hidden so that enemies will not find it.

The duck likes to build her nest near water, but with so many houses and roads around, she has a hard time finding a place. Sometimes she has to use the branches of a tree or a hole in its trunk. When she finds the right place, she begins to build her nest with twigs and reeds. She lines it with the soft down feathers of her underfeathers. Then she lays her eggs.

The duck sits on, or broods, her eggs for a month. She keeps them warm so that the duckling inside the egg will grow. When she leaves the nest to find food, she carefully covers the eggs with feathers, stalks of grass and small twigs. She does not want any enemies to notice the nest while she is away and the eggs are unprotected.

When the duck hears a strange noise, she backs off her eggs slowly. As soon as she feels safe, she goes back to brooding.

Here we see what is happening inside an egg. A little duckling is beginning to grow.

2nd day: An almost invisible group of cells, called an embryo, will grow into a duckling in about four weeks. The embryo swims in the yellow yolk, its source of food and nourishment.

4th day: Already the head of the duckling (showing the outline of the brain) and the body, which has not yet grown any limbs, can be seen.

 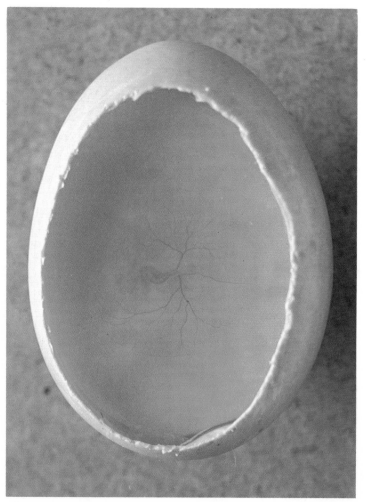

A tiny speck beats inside the body. This is the heart. It is connected to a system of blood vessels through which the embryo breathes and digests food from the yolk.

6th day: The embryo has grown and the blood vessels have developed too. The small black dot is the eye's retina. Limbs are beginning to form.

10th day: The embryo has grown bigger. The ear is seen as a little patch directly behind the eye. Birds do not have ears like ours. Their eardrums open directly onto the surface of the head.

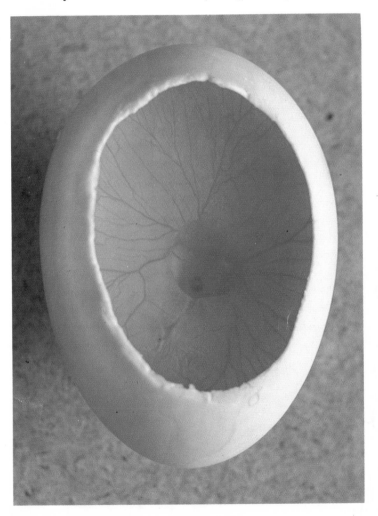

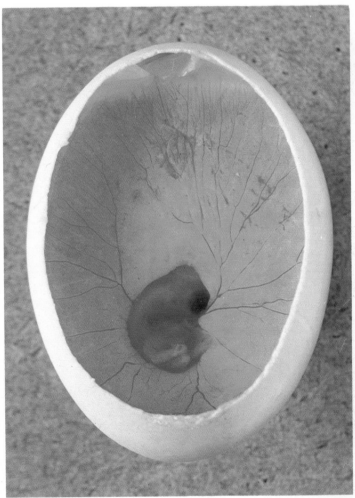

14th day: Now we can see clearly the duckling's body and its long beak. Feathers have appeared.

At the tip of the duckling's beak is a chalky, hard, diamond-shaped growth which the duckling will use to break out of its shell. The shell is thinner now because part of it has been used to make the duckling's bones.

20th day: The duckling fills most of the space inside the egg. The yolk is much smaller because the nourishment it contained has been fed into the duckling through the blood vessels.

26th day: The duckling is still connected to the yolk by a cord of blood vessels, but it is ready to hatch out of its egg.

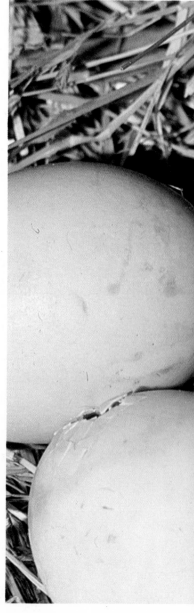

So much has happened inside the egg. As the duckling begins to move around, it hammers at the eggshell with the hard growth at the tip of its beak. A hole is made. The duckling moves and stretches. The shell begins to crack.

Suddenly the egg splits in two and the duckling is out of the egg. His feathers are wet and his eyes blink in the bright light. It has been so dark inside the egg.

The little duckling is weak and tired, but the fresh air is good to breathe and the warm sunshine quickly dries his feathers.

Within an hour, the duckling looks bold and perky. He is ready to explore the world. As soon as his feathers dry, he can follow his mother into the water.

The duckling and his brothers and sisters walk in a row, one after another behind their mother, to a lake. They are not afraid, but their mother stretches her long neck and looks about.

She is looking for enemies, but they have come to a safe place. If there is any danger, she can hide her ducklings in the reeds in the shallow water near the shore.

The first little duckling has already followed his mother into the water. He swims and dives easily and soon all the ducklings are in the water. They learn quickly that good things to eat are just beneath the surface of the water—green weeds, water plants and small insects.

On land the ducklings cheep in their high-pitched duckling voices. One day they will sound more like their mother and father whose low quacking echoes across the water—"yeeb, yeeb."

The family swims together, although the drake no longer has much interest in the duck and her brood of ducklings. Now and then he takes charge of the young, but he likes to stay at a distance while they swim about for food.

Within two months the ducklings' soft down feathers will turn into flight feathers. They will be able to fly like their parents and travel over meadows and fields. Their world is full of natural and man-made dangers, but ducks have been known to live as long as eighteen years.

In only one month a duckling has grown inside an egg and hatched out into a new world. Soon he will go off on his own and one day he too will grow splendid bright feathers in the fall and find a mallard duck with which to spend the winter.